WOMAN IN RAINLIGHT

WOMAN
IN RAINLIGHT

Poems by

Jean Tupper

HOBBLEBUSH BOOKS

ISBN: 0-9760896-0-2
Library of Congress Control Number: 2004113126

Composed at Hobblebush Books,
Brookline, New Hampshire

Printed in the United States of America

Text and titles are composed in Bembo, a serene face of true Renaissance structure produced by Monotype in 1929, based on a roman cut at Venice by Francisco Griffo in 1495.

Cover: Watercolor by Linda Saunders, Chatham, MA

Published by:
Hobblebush Books

17-A Old Milford Road
Brookline, New Hampshire 03033
www.hobblebush.com

ACKNOWLEDGMENTS

Grateful acknowledgment is made to the editors and publishers of the following publications in which poems in this collection have appeared (sometimes in earlier versions), or will appear.

Blue Unicorn: "Captiva"
Carquinez Poetry Review: "Wite-Out"
Confluence: "Mama's Pillbox"
The Connecticut Writer: "Seismology of Love"
The Distillery: "In the Dentist's Chair"
The Larcom Review: "Papa's Knot"
The MacGuffin: "Crossing the Ompompanoosuc"
The Madison Review: "Shrink Art"
The Nebraska Review: "Mother of the Bride"
New Delta Review: "Looking for Bali"
Paterson Literary Review: "Mother Nasty"
Piedmont Literary Review: "Flannel Sheets"
Poetpourri (now *The Comstock Review*): "Taking CPR"
RE:AL: "The Name I Give Myself"
Rio Grande Review: "She Hates to Complain but . . ."
Sanskrit Literary-Arts Magazine: "Wite-Out"
Schuylkill Valley Journal of the Arts: "Rain"
Solo: "What I Found in Mama's Black Leather Bag . . ."
Southern Humanities Review: "Riding the Pumpkin Coach with Mum"
Southern Poetry Review: "Raccoons, the Most Articulate"
Thema: "Timid Lady Rides the Redline"
Tunxis Poetry Review: "Ladybug" and "Facing the Phonetics of Fear,"
   "Firm Pulls Make Strong Cables," "Mama's Chowder"
Voices International: "Pink"
Worcester Review: "Quahogging with Uncle Windy"
West Wind Review: "When Your Father Died"
Wisconsin Review: "January"

New Moon Poetry Contest Winner, 2000: "House for Sale"
Joseph H. Brodine Contest: "The Word-Sifter Sails off the Mountain"

SPECIAL THANKS to Susan Deborah King, longtime friend and poet, who was an unfailing source of encouragement that this book might come into existence and be shared with others; to my trusted ms. readers,

Patricia Fargnoli and J.Lorraine Brown; and to my daughter, Nancy
Tupper Ling, who provided technical assistance as well as moral support.

I also want to thank the Wood Thrush Poets (who have been my
sisters in poetry for twenty-five years) and Fine Line Poets, for the gift
of their encouragement and critiques, and my family, especially Russ, for
his neverending support.

Additional thanks to Donald Sheehan and the Frost Place, where
some of these poems were nourished, and to those dedicated teachers,
like Miss Kent, who encouraged me to write in the first place.

Other poets—Brendan Galvin, Paul Zimmer, Heather McHugh,
Laure-Anne Bosselaar, Gail Mazur, Melanie Braverman, Martha Rhodes,
Robert Cording, Suzanne Cleary, Ted Deppe, Renée Ashley—helped in
ways even they might be surprised to know.

For Russ

CONTENTS

LITTLE MOTHER

LOOKING FOR BALI

WOMAN IN RAINLIGHT

EARLY LESSONS

. . . the chowder could simmer, but it was not allowed to curdle or boil . . .

—Mama's Chowder

FIRM PULLS MAKE STRONG CABLES

Casting on those rose-colored stitches,
Mother, your patterns emerge
in twisted checks and double-woven ribs.
A few still fit, like sweaters to backs
and backs to burdens. Others are
nubby or threadbare now.

I used to watch you gather strands for
Little Butterfly, or spin to Fair Isles.
Some of your styles were simple,
like Sand and Moss. I wore them
for sunburn coverups, for shivers
of picnics in White Mountain glens,
for sleepover weekends with
stogie-fed uncles and hard-candy aunts.

Later I puzzled over your fretwork—
all those three-twisted mock ribbings
for a brassy teenage pullover—
I just wanted to buy the one in Sam's window,
but your needles clicked their boned fury.
You hummed your soprano and wove
your hymns into the mesh, while I struggled
to untangle the web of yarns at your feet.

Now, like a Slipped Hourglass, you are gone.
More than the patterns, I miss
the background stitches—so many purled loops—
and all the heathery shades in your basket.
Ripping back through all those rows, I see
you never minded the unravelings.
Sometimes I even lift your proverbs,
like sweaters from mothballed boxes.

WRITING IT DOWN

the way I emblazon my name
on Virginia Peachey's front steps
with my cherry-berry crayon
at the birthday party
when I am six, preferring
my own block print letters
to pin-the-tail-on-the-donkey
in her back yard

how, when everyone comes
laughing and clapping,
they find me
with my flamboyant
sideshow — and see
what I can do —

but mama insists
it's a terrible thing,
even though she knows
I meant no harm
and only wanted
to make her proud

even now my face
remembers the burn
of having to go back
with her good lye soap
and a heavy brush,
to scrub off the letters
that spell me

LADYBUG

Little turtle-back,
scarab with wings
that flutter 70 times
while I blink—
I like your fashionable
raincoat! This season's
copper-brown laminate
with black polka-dots
suits you:
the mini-Martian
with bentwire legs,
filament-thin
zigzagging life's
horizontal sheets
and ascending the vertical
glass of my window.

I can only imagine
your sensilla and antennae,
those tactile hairs on your
palps and tarsi
that hear and touch
the song and fuzz
of aphids on a stem,
and your eye
that scans for images
(but often misses red)
sees patterns
of ultraviolet
reflections on flowers—
a garden I will never see.

QUAHOGGING WITH
UNCLE WINDY

It is always Sunday morning.
The sun is shining
and I am eleven, jumpskipping
behind you, sinking deep
in your sandy tracks
as we head for Yarmouth Bay
with our buckets and rakes.

We wade in up to ankles,
then knees, and shivers
go rippling like waves.
I would be afraid of you,
the big plaid-shirt man
with hornpout mouth,
if you were not my uncle.

But I know that
neither of us can swim
that well, and we will
only go out to your suspenders
and then begin feeling around
with our rakes and toes
for the right bumps,

happy because
our feet are doing
this underwater dance
that is invisible
to passersby,
and we are filling our buckets
with the clink and clunk
of living stones.

SPRING COMES IN CRAYOLA COLORS

I'm scooping pointless mayo off
my filet-o-fish at McDonald's,
thinking of my age,
when the bright colors grab me.
Someone's taped up this class work.
Crayola drawings, ceiling high, circle the room.
The children's "Spring"—these first-grade
impressions of robins and kites—
dance over me. There are
heart-red tulips and tulip-red hearts
stuck on lime-green stems. There are ducks,
swimming in azure. Kathy's are either
very large ducks in a small pond
or paddlers in a puddle.
Raymond's don't swim yet.

Something about creamy-vanilla paper
carries me back to a hard seat
in Miss McIntyre's room . . .
I'm watching her count out the sheets
and lick her fingers to get the exactly-right
number per row; and I'm front seat,
so pretty soon I've got mine and I'm
bearing down hard with canary—
till my waxy sun-ball is big enough,
and the flame-orange spokes are spinning
like pinwheels. They blaze down
on my house, which is just four walls
and a pup-tent roof, but I always
add a chimney—every house needs
a fireplace and burning logs inside;
and I think it needs a fruit tree, with two
or three ruby-red apples (big as grapefruit),
and a rainbow, with every color
bent like golden arches
running off the page.

MAMA'S CHOWDER

Mama always stirred the soup
or roux clockwise to pinwheels,
as steam curled her dark
hair to tendrils.

She could sing or talk
faster than her fish fumet
bubbled, with its creamy cubes
of potato and chips of onion.

Adding milk,
she hummed warnings
to the chowder and me.
If you knew her hymns
you could lift
lines of admonition,
like covers from kettles.

The chowder could simmer
but it was not allowed
to curdle or boil;
"Love Divine" was lagniappe,
the butcher's gift of fish heads
thrown in with a soup "bunch"
that cost a nickel.

Even now, reduced
to Pritikin formulas
for heart or hypertension
and thickening with
grated raw potato
instead of cream,

she makes it taste good:
seasons with dill or tarragon
and ladles the piping-hot
chowder from her old tureen
into my well-heated bowl.

PAPA'S KNOT

That summer when he was seventeen
Papa, who's always been a hard worker,
sweated it out at Mr. Bird's company

which when he was growing up
in that Massachusetts town was the one
to work for. Everyone worked there, his dad too.

It got its name from Charlie, the #1 Bird man,
who made his first million in paper.
The rest came later, from roofing and shingles.

Papa slaved in "the box shop" that summer
and the next, which as he tells it meant
hot as blazes, something always coming at you

on that conveyer belt: hundreds of boxes,
folded down and stacked up, twenty-five to a batch.
That's how his fingers learned to lasso a stack

of flattened cartons with twine *on the double*
and the trick which now, 65 years later,
he wants to pass on like an heirloom

because he still remembers the box shop knot
and thinks someone else in the family
should know how to tie it.

FACING THE PHONETICS OF FEAR

Only yesterday the soft G of geranium
and hydrangea swirled over me
in this borrowed cottage by the sea,
where gentle winds once whistled
us to sleep like children.
But tonight, after midnight,
as the tide rises,
winds gasp and moan,
mount a dark and moonless sky.
A sudden gust rides the rooftop,
riffles shingles and sails them
off in a tempest that sandblasts
my windows, shivers my sills.

As junipers hug the ground
I clutch my pillow and watch
the frenzy of wind-whipped pines
flinging shadows at shutters:
their rage explodes on my bedroom wall.
The little cottage begins to lift
and sway on its foundation,
groaning and shaking me
from my bed with guttural sounds
that mimic the hard G of Gog and Magog—
while something glabrous and glassy-eyed
glares from the folds at my window,
refuses to be a curtain till dawn.

BURNING IS BANNED HERE

Who will remember the smell of leaves burning?
Raking and bagging I think these leaves
are like people — so many shriveled up
pieces of brown and gray
that used to be ruddy as Aunt Elvie,
who could turn them into mountains
for me to jump over or into feet first.
Then she'd hand the rake to my uncle,
her scowling, tight-lipped Windy,
and light the match.

Where have the pungent fires of my childhood gone?
If they still lie smoldering somewhere down under
these leaves, I want the first smoky wisps
to rise from these heaps and thicken
to umber fog, even as I want the ashen faces
of the dying aunts and uncles
to redden again, like these sugar maples.

Let me sniff the old, remembered
brown-acid scent that frightens the little hairs in my nose,
scratches my throat, and makes me cry:
for Aunt Elvie who died last Spring;
and for the gruff uncle who just had a bypass
and finally dared to tell me his secret.
I love you. You're like a daughter to me.

LOVE–SHAPES

. . . the room, the air . . . smelling of lilacs.
—The Dance

SEISMOLOGY OF LOVE

Sometimes you can see it all
in the yellow blink of a cat's eye
or flutter of feathers.

Some things soft and small
cling to your mind
like thistles on socks.

Caring, you might see
in summer's smile
a newly-seeded storm:

track, like a Richter,
by tremble of lip,
recent rumblings and quake.

Love reads all the hurt
in slight arch of brow.
Some sighs are sonic booms.

PINK

After these six days
it will always be Bermuda:
blushing houses on a hill,
the rosy talc of sand,
and that first hibiscus—
your gift, surprising my pillow.
At Mangrove Bay, the bougainvillea—
drenching the limestone wall and
dancing past a small ballerina
learning arabesques
that Saturday morning
in Somerset—
matching the hot color
of her lips and tights.
And your face, a pink sun,
pouring its warmth
down on me,
my cheeks burning.

RAIN

It begins in an August twilight   *Let it begin gently* I say

a gentle rain   as we lie sleepless in our bed

at last. After many parched days   the thing we've been waiting for

the air is wet: Wake up, stones! Wake up to the passion of rain

the leaves are licking their lips   and touching each other tenderly

Even the oaks are happy . . .   *arousal* is the word that comes to mind

as brown edges green up again.   The rain is stroking everything

It sprinkles the night   with sensual syncopation.

It fills my darkened room   It fills me with its pizzicato

and I think: I can live without stars.   This rainlight is enough for me.

It breathes softly in my ear   It showers me with kisses . . . kisses everywhere

and I think: I can live without moon.   This wetness is making me shine.

FLANNEL SHEETS

These winters in New England
you have to have them
to get you through.
Ours are blue
to match the walls
and patchwork quilt.

They keep us
warm as bears
in hibernation—
except for noses,
which of course remain
outside at 50°.

The problem is pajamas
if you wear them, and if
they are flannel. Flannel
on flannel in a kingsized
bed is paddling upstream.

You can curl up
like a cocoon—but
more often you are a moth,
with wings attached
to butter.

I am often reminded of
Mary, Joseph, and the lambs
in Sunday school—
those felt figures,
pressed to flannel boards,
stuck so well
we couldn't peel them off.

Even our dreams
are rubber cement.
I can never do
a proper pirouette,
and he never slides
into third base on time.
You can't fly on flannel.

SOMETHING OF ME
GOES WITH YOU

I help you pack everything
into the old black footlocker—
scratched, mothballed—
it went to college years ago with me.
You hate my sewing the labels
that name your sweaters
and vests—hoping
to ward off future losses.

You stuff in
what's important:
the Gashlycrumb poster
of tiny horrors,
etched and alphabetized
by Edward Gorey:
A is for Amy
who fell down the stairs,
B is for Basil,
assaulted by bears . . .

your whistling teakettle;
bedraggled Pooh;
and all those underlining
pens and pencils,
ready to smear old Chancellor
Bismarck in *couleur de rose,*
to paint Malvolio
in his yellow socks.

I can see you burning
under a gooseneck,
aiming crumpled wads

at this black plastic
hole in the night.
I do not envy you
the tests, the clammy
palms and skipbeat heart;
but I could wish each day,
like you, to sign my name
on fresh white sheets.

MOTHER OF THE BRIDE

A week to go.
I laugh. I cry. My head throbs.
Don't slam the door . . . I'll scream.
She's going to MARRY him!
Can't sort it out.
My computer disk is muddled.
Where's the Guest List?
Index won't tell me who's coming:
WEDDSTUF only leads to
dishes and flatware;
WEDDLIST takes me back
to rented tuxedos, forgotten DJ's
and the Cake Lady of Rehobeth,
who came with her double-rich
chocolate devils and plainwhite layers,
laced with an orange squeeze
or hint of almond. Then dropped
her tales of fluttery brides—
and a runaway groom!

In a nightmare my gargantuan corsage
pulls me down, and a sharp hatpin
stabs my chest, reminding me
My baby's going to be married!
Tomorrow I must tell Bruce the florist
all I want is a single fuchsia rose
to match my wedding suit. Still
sleepless at 5 AM I tiptoe out of doors,
discover the consummate rose
"Pink Elegance" is climbing my neighbor's fence,
and convince myself she'd want me to have it.
Anyway, it isn't me, it's someone else—
the clown, the sleepwalker—

who snips off that rose with frantic
fingernails. Tells herself
It's for Bruce. He needs to know!
waves it wildly in his face and tells him
Won't it be perfect? with a little baby's breath?

THE DANCE *or*
WHY I STILL WALK
AT THE STATE SCHOOL

Retardation: a wall that is incomplete
and will always stand half-built.

His name was John.
He was a resident, and some days
as I pass the crumbling buildings
I think what a grand place this used to be
and wonder if he still lives.

As a reporter my job was to get the story—
show them dancing, having fun.
I'd mastered a few definitions
but hadn't lived them yet.
In April, as I orbit the state school,
I smell the lilacs and think of John.

Forty years ago:
the photographer is worried.
Can he only take the backs
of heads? Are faces taboo?
"Shots from the balcony won't cut it,"
he says. "Gotta hit the dance floor."

I feel all jittery—afraid.
What if someone asks me to dance?
How could I refuse? What would it be like
to do the twist—or even a foxtrot—
with someone here?

Of course it happens.
Black hair slicked back like Elvis,

white bucks, red tie, tweed jacket
flapping open as he approaches,
kind of panting—dark eyes smiling,
breath like peppermint candy—

he taps me on the arm
and I can see he's just as
sweaty and nervous as I,
both of us trembling, but his
hands and feet know what to do.
We swing out onto the dance floor,
he counting the steps, holding me
with determination and obvious pleasure,
the room, the air . . . smelling of lilacs.

MISHOO

She drops Bippa, her favorite bear,
runs to open the door,
and pulls me in (kiss, kiss).

That's how it is
when we come together.

After five years waiting,
thinking she would never be,
she *is*. She's Elizabeth,
who just turned two, and I'm
the greedy grandmother,
who wants more time
with this precious
first and only.

After a month's separation,
she comes midweek for a
three-day visit with her parents.

It's never enough.
Already I know when she leaves
the house will be too quiet—

no more jabbering—
just waiting for the phone
to ring: *mishoonana.*

TOUJOURS L'AMOUR

I'm looking hard at the silky
silver your fingers comb through
absentmindedly, as you cull
news from newspapers.

If I could count those hairs—
still cut short and boyishly
parted, the separate strands
now thinning in some places—

or drift into a trance
that restores the chestnut
fire and smoke we knew,
perhaps I could salvage

something: a line
to outlast the ashes of death,
the collapse of buildings
and brain cells.

LOSS

. . . the angel's wing is bent, the old felt bear needs stitching . . .
—Untrimming the Tree

JANUARY

"Life's too much for ordinary mortals."
—*Mary Tyler*

Everything's falling apart,
right down to the handle
on the front door
that broke off this morning
like an icicle;

but the blue spruce
on this New England deck,
wrapped, roots and all, in burlap,
was our choice: *a living tree*
to drape in multi-colored lights
for Christmas. Now under siege,
her branches look like arms
weighed down in sorrow,
from the weight of many snows.

In a fresh blizzard
tree drifts like the ghost
of a white ship in a white-out
and vanishes beneath
billowing waves of snow;
but somewhere down under
this sea tonight: a muffled glow,
like the memory of light.

UNTRIMMING THE TREE

Putting away the Christmas
tree ornaments, I sit with my cup
of lemon lift tea, now scanning
this week's *Time*, now tucking away
Snoopy and the red trolls,
with their small green packages
and double-runnered sleds.

I see the angel's wing is bent,
the old felt bear needs stitching
and—on page 65 of the magazine—
another plane is down.
The popcorn is my childhood,
strung next to Cape Cod cranberries,
when life was simple as this
Scherenschnitte paper doll.

A few satin balls still tremble
on the bluespruce as I wrap
the straw lady and fragile ornaments
in tissue to keep them safe
for another year, and flip past
that human ornament—a child—
dangling from a tree on the next page.

Little skaters skim over
my frosted mirror. Little singers
stand gaping under a dim lamp.
I know I can stitch the old brown bear.
I know I can fix the angel's wing,
but who will mend the broken child
lost on a Christmas flight?

IN THE DENTIST'S CHAIR

Just because everything's crumbling—
(your filling fell out at lunch!
you hid it in a napkin)
you should not have to make excuses
to this freckle-faced kid, your dentist,
who is naturally less concerned
about your deteriorating bicuspid
than he is about the house he's building
Excuse me, the architect's calling!
and the hors d'oeuvres they served
at the party last night (yum-yum!)
which he's discussing with Rae,
his pretty red-haired assistant . . . and now
they're going on about her night-blooming cereus?

It's hard to defend yourself when you're
tied up in a chair like this—feet up, head down—
with a masked man and his sidekick discussing
fiber optics or the latest invasion somewhere,
and all you can see is their eyes—
his are green, hers are brown—
and all you can do is nod YES or NO,
should they ask your opinion,
which they don't very often—
your job is just to *Open wide!* and
Wider please! so he can get in your mouth,
and hers is to mop up the fallen chunks
of silver inside . . . and the drool
when it runs down your chin.

You don't know when. You're numb.
Right now your tongue can't tell

the inside of your cheek from a dinner roll.
It just tastes the treacherous clove and
licks the place where the needle went in.
Inside your mouth feels dry and stiff
as a box with a cardboard lip;
and the only other wet thing
is your left eye, which has a mind of its own
and weeps uncontrollably —
like Papa's after the stroke, weeping for all
the numbed and numbing world.

WHEN YOUR FATHER DIED

for my husband

Wind howling over
the black limo, all of us
waxed and polished. The lineup:
winding, unwinding itself
in death, as noonday shoppers
freeze in our light.

Nodding heads,
snapdragons and gladioli,
shaking over his casket.

The widow: pearls and black
shantung. *Keep a stiff lip.*
This code — the legacy —
she passes to her son,
the latest spit-shined child
to sail these waves.

HOUSE FOR SALE

I remember when new love
painted the baby's crib with a flourish,
and a daughter's birth announcement.
Yes, there was a baby in this house,
and the house and the baby were
surprising as the tulips and dahlias
he planted each year, to see if I'd notice.

Now, after 25 years, he's painted
a sign: FOR SALE BY OWNER
and planted it on our front lawn,
naming this new event in our lives;
and I wonder what else he's ramming
into the ground with his sharp stakes
and heavy I-beam. Is he lost

as I am in this maple tree
memory of a sapling we gave each other
the year we couldn't replace our loss?
Could only watch that baby tree grow
till it covered our barren lawn with green
branches and red-gold flutterings
we ache from raking each fall.

MOVING

The February chill
and I'm bone-tired,
drifting back and forth
between body and mind—

days and miles spent straddling
two lives and two houses;
packing, unpacking
boxes in a dinky red trailer.

My stomach and the wash
in a perpetual spin, a tear
in my left eye; my right
a red-lined roadmap.

I ask myself which house?
Which state? Can't find anything.
Where's the damn crockpot
to make a good stew?

THE LONELY DRAGON

Can't get used to this place.
New house. New town.
No one knows me yet.
Don't like the way my voice
bounces here: from hardwood floors
to high ceilings; then echoes
back from cups and saucers
so loud even my whispers scare me.
New house doesn't know my footsteps
or remember my fragrance—jasmine;
and she smells too new, too clean—
except on rainy days, when there's a
pungent whiff of wet paint and plaster.

These days I'm so whacky
I peep through my own peephole.
Imagine friends stopping by,
ringing my doorbell. Or ring it
myself—just to hear it ring.
If they should catch me
I'll tell them I'm testing
for sound—or trying to avoid
the red eyes of a burglar
system that scans my every move.
And if they should notice
a kind of vaporous breathing
that fills my chimney with
new smoke and fear, I'll tell them
it's the dragon, the resident dragon.
Sometimes he sighs—hot sighs
that quiver my lashes, make me weep.

TAKING CPR

The dummies are bedraggled:
the big one we call Gus has a ripped-open mouth
from too many tongue-jaw thrusts;
the little lady we call Annie
has a permanently distorted midriff
and bleached-out look, from too many washings;
the child's head comes off.

We're bedraggled too:
one bad back, a major headache
and several cases of sniffles
hyperventilate in this classroom.
My own throat is scratchy;
I think maybe I'll just pass out
and let someone practice on me.
But I can't do that—not tonight.

Tonight's the test: mouth to mouth.
All the jokes about stiffs and wakes
seem less funny now. We have to mount
these dummies: blow them back to life.
Everyone puffs his capful of wind;
delivers abdominal Heimlichs and
hot rescue breaths to victims,
conscious and un-,

I kneel beside the fallen woman,
blow my first hesitant breath,
then wait . . . for lungs to expand.
This isn't Annie any more. It's Mama.
I shiver for fear her chest won't rise
or I'll crush her delicate bones.
The big man isn't Gus tonight either.
It's you, love. I count seconds.
Pray I can make this mannequin breathe.

MISSING YOU

You were always quick
to listen to my life,
to put yourself in the picture
I had just taken
of manatees
drifting to sleep
in the Caloosahatchee,
to stroke the
angulate wentletrap
I carried home to you
from Sanibel.

Even when you could no longer travel
and winter was at your doorstep
you savored my telescopic shots
of bottlenose dolphins
of roseate spoonbills
as if you'd been there
and snapped them yourself.

Which is why
I can't get used to your not being here
and miss you more than ever
when I come home from being
somewhere else.

LITTLE MOTHER

. . . her wee hunched body teetering on the edge . . .

—Mama's Pillbox

LITTLE FOX

Maybe you can guess this face
was always pretty,
and there's a smidge of vanity
in that Petite Sophisticate
which claims no more than 80
pounds or years —
goes to bed in a steam-pressed
negligée, and wakes at five . . . *pouf!*
all rosy and color-coordinated,
with scarf to match.

If she calls, her story takes off
breakneck. I'm lost,
and the devil himself can't follow
her twists and hairpin turns.
Tonight she drowns me out
and my guardian angel is
off duty, so Lucifer rides
and I call her the champion of
(don't let her hear this!)
chatterbabblewit.

But you should never underestimate
Mother-power: the force
that can spot your lie in a whisper
or fever at arm's length;
and yet if one of her old truths is missing,
Mother invents a new one.
In a voice scratchy with love
and pain, she'll hit you
with Canticles 2:15 and . . . *Presto!* YOU
are one of those "little foxes" that spoil the vines.

Canticles is also called *The Song of Solomon.*

MOTHER DOT GETS NEW
ROSE-COLORED SHADES

She grabs one of the cords
and fiddles with it till
the insulated honeycombs dance
up and down—
there was that little space
maybe a hair's width?
didn't you notice? on the far edge
between the window and frame?
through which, she claimed,
the boogeyman's been peeking in
at her in her thin nightie,
craving a better look
at the fallen bosom she hoists up
and tucks into lace cups each morning.

All *bravissima* now
that her rosy shades are up
and she's outfoxed Peeping Tom,
she floats back to her John Hancock days,
when sweet young things
of ample proportions like herself
were invited to meet the boss
on the eighth floor for "special assignments."
Of course I never went
she declares, hands on hips,
daring me to doubt her story.

Funny though, how the eighth floor
keeps coming up, and all the men
have faces and names.
My role is small: to sympathize,
"Poor you . . . lucky me,"

only half believing my good fortune
at never having been squeezed *there*
by assorted uncles and strangers;
and she, putting a hand to her famous *buzzoom,*
tells me how hard it's been to carry
that heavy burden all her life.

Then she converts her cane to a saber
and gives one of the new shades
a fierce, Napoleonic yank that shoots it to the top —
proving she's in charge and she alone
will decide when this curtain goes up.

MAMA'S PILLBOX

She laughs with a little a-ha!
her sassy Alice-blue eyes
scanning the labels:

her wee hunched body
teetering on the edge
of the white crocheted bedspread,

her bent fingers determined
to line up the arrows
and pop the caps off a dozen pill bottles.

Dumping, spreading, sorting
the capsules and caplets
that decorate her table and bed,

she studies the colors and shapes
dancing before her with child eyes, as if
something interesting is sure to happen,

and introduces me to a newcomer, Levoxyl,
the tiniest pill in her pillbox.
Isn't she a beauty?

I have to admit—palest peach,
shaped like a butterfly—it's true,
never mind how tiny;

but she's drifted
to Isosorbide's soft yellow—it's
the color of a prom dress she once wore—

and "that skinny red Altace"
It's for heart you know!
makes her think of a high school romance.

She prattles on,
now fingering a shiny orb
that looks like a pearl,

now shrinking before my eyes.
Unfazed, she tweezes each tidbit
into the plastic compartments of old age

and makes a game of it,
subdividing her weeks into days,
days into morning, noon and night.

SHE HATES TO
COMPLAIN BUT . . .

At 85, she tries hard
to remember
what restaurant? what town?

"There was someone
in the next booth
with a face

like a friend." The friend
was ———— (Henry?)
Town was ———— (Cornish?)

Papa fills in her blanks.
Every morning and night,
this Wheel-of-Fortune.

Now she's cold.
"Get the nitro . . .
there's a pain in my heart."

Bones are achey.
Nails are splitting.
"This house is falling apart."

MOTHER NASTY

is after me again.
She's been eating
her redhot pepper pills

and the devil
pops out of her
medicine kit

with an idea that's
really twisted,
devious

something she just
remembered
I did as a little girl

like wetting my pants
and coming home from
school with chapped legs

or burying
the book I threw up on
in the backyard.

Now she's telling
everyone at the beauty shop
my age —*Doesn't my little girl*

look young for 60?—
all the while
she's sticking pins in

her Jeanie voodoo doll.
My head feels like
that old man's in church

that never stops bobbing
up and down, up and down.
I'm shaking inside too

like the flu's got me —
first the chills,
then dizzying hot waves.

It's sick how
she loves and hates
at the same time:

clings and squeezes
the life out of me
with her love tentacles

then walks over me
like an army of red ants,
stinging my flesh raw.

If she really loved me
wouldn't she
make me some wings?

Stitch them with
her finest needles?
Lift me with her blessings as I fly?

RIDING THE PUMPKIN COACH WITH MUM

"I had a dream which was not all a dream."
—*Lord Byron*

I'm waiting for the elevator door to open,
planning to meet friends at an upper level,
but as I enter Mama appears
with her Scottish plaid, crotchety look
and we take off on this strange, bumpy ride
at which point I realize the elevator
is actually a detachable unit or vehicle,
something like Cinderella's pumpkin coach
or a carnival ride out of my past.
It travels on a special upsy-downsy track
that moves in its own convoluted fashion
with her steering the rig, at first rolling along
at a reasonable rate, before accelerating
to a high speed—like a rollercoaster
I rode once as a child at Nantasket Beach—
the sudden drop forcing my head back
till my neck feels like it might break off.
Then a fantastic scene comes into view
in paradisal colors, more Day-glo than life:
shimmering hills and lush valleys
beckon as Sarah Brightman sings
"Time to Say Goodbye" and we zoom
to a halt. It's the end of the line
so the old lady—my mother—hops out,
expecting me to do the same, but I
drop her off with a gruff "Gotta go now!"
jump back in the magical coach and take off
for another look at that gorgeous scene.
Out of the corner of my eye I see
she's shaking her fist at me for abandoning her
and casting a spell as she trots down the path
to her gingerbread house,
like the witch in *Hansel and Gretel*.

SHRINK ART

This is about the little mother
who is shrinking, shrinking
so her skirts keep falling down
everywhere we go . . .
even the ones with elastic bands
are falling down now.

And this is the woman
who once knew how
to sew a fine seam,
and can still thread a needle
and take a tuck here and there
and does, but even so
her skirts keep falling down.

WHAT I FOUND IN MAMA'S
BLACK LEATHER BAG
THE WEEK AFTER SHE DIED

A small bottle of Estée Lauder's "Cinnabar"
for dabs behind the ear.
What's a woman without her scent?

A handkerchief with a lace edge
tatted by an ancient aunt.
Ladies don't use kleenex!

A ballpoint from an Ossipee bank,
attached to her checkbook as usual,
with string and elastic, so as not

to lose itself in this black interior.
The little scissors, sharp and curved;
and the tweezers she toted

to pluck stray chin hairs
as we drove to *Hair & Beyond*
for a morning of beautification.

A note, from her sweetheart of 62 years,
lying deep in this widow's purse
next to some of her favorite texts:

Behold, thou art fairest among women.
And here is her wallet, stuffed with
family photos, all secured in their

plastic sheaths. She used them
like credit cards, to buy something
intangible. We were her cachet.

I finger her hairbrush,
the one with the ivory handle papa shortened
to fit her pocketbook. The bristles

still clutch a few strands,
pearly with White Minx rinse.
I pull them off and roll them in my palm—

a silvery ball that seems to move
with the pulsebeat of my hand—the only
part of her little body still with me and shining.

LOOKING FOR BALI

. . . because we had used up all the time we had . . .
—Looking for Bali

THE NAME I GIVE MYSELF

is Blue.
Not skyblue or aster.
Past midlife, I'm not pastel
and cerulean's too angelic
for me now. Only in dreams
do I wrap myself in a peacock
serape . . . or wear
the indigo bunting's vest.

No. My blue is *tsunami.*
A rain-soaked seawave
undersea. A volcanic quake
with downpour of molten blue
ocean drenching my frazzled
blue hair. A volley of blue-black
thunderclaps . . . collapsing
the turquoise of my inner ear.

Mine is the midnight blue
of threads running helterskelter
all over my conscience. The cobalt
blue of spiderveins rushing down my
legs. The bloodshot-blue of
my own eyes . . . staring back
from a broken glass.

WITE-OUT

Rather than cross out *fait accompli*
items on your To Do List
with inky Bic or black magic
that invariably bleeds through
to the next page and makes it look
even more thick and threatening
than the original commands,
why not make them disappear?

What you do is buy a little bottle
of super-white, super-smooth
cleanup fluid, the goop that promises
to make all the corrections you need.
Unscrew the top and start painting over
assignments you've hated for months,
names that gave you heartburn.
Slather gobs on ex- dastardly deeds.

You slap the white stuff on everything
you're done with, or want to be.
Make white clouds all over the page,
covering bills you've decided not to pay,
RSVPs you won't respond to.
Pretty soon, white to the knuckles,
you're loving the absence of
demanding things and people.

Eradication empowers. Your mood
lightens and pressure drops as you
whiten up. You're the artist,
adding white space; the domestic
engineer, uncluttering closets. Or, like me,
you're Lady Macbeth, "Out, out ... "
removing those treacherous spots
till there's nothing left but white on white.

CROSSING THE
OMPOMPANOOSUC

To me it is *nouvelle musique,*
this river with five syllables
rushing beneath the bridge and
ending in *oosuc,* which even
untranslated tells me something
of its birth, Indian and watery,
calling to my fear of the deep
and wet, till I am crossing and re-
crossing that old trestle bridge,
high and dangerously slatted
over fast water . . .
me holding my breath,
you holding my hand,
but even then I am afraid
to look down.

TIMID LADY RIDES
THE REDLINE

"The people are a many-headed beast."
—*Horace*

She shudders at
sudden vibrations

clutches her
Aigner bag

for the
dark tunnel

subway screech
and T-stop

at Kendall Square.
An eyeblink

as her car emerges
in noonday sun.

She studies feet,
the intentions of

scuffed sandals,
cruel boots. Even

in this better light
her downcast eyes

wary, scanning
scurrilous pantlegs,

frayed seams . . .
only pretending

to read the gentle
poems in her lap:

Some Beasts
by Pablo Neruda,

crossing over
Longfellow Bridge.

LOOKING FOR BALI

Today we gave up blueberry pancakes,
at least the idea of having them
this morning for breakfast,
because we had used up all the time we had
searching for Bali. I thought
we should look it up —
at least know where it is
longitudinally and latitudinally,
and maybe something more
so I'm flipping through the dictionary
under the B's to find out,
east of Java, an island,
population three million,
so I won't have to wait for the next
blowoup or TV report
to be sure it's east of Jakarta,
which at least I do know
is the capital; because if terrorists
insist on blowing up hotels
in Bali — and elsewhere — it behooves us
to be able to spin the globe
to Indonesia and put a finger on it,
but I can't seem to find it.
So I reach for the big Rand McNally
atlas, and keep my finger moving
east of Java . . . but where is it?
Can't seem to find those four little letters
on the map, the ones I'm looking for,
only the Bali Sea, which as it turns out
is somewhere else. But now I'm jubilant
because the index is pointing me to

G6 and I can see why I couldn't find it before,
since Bali has somehow gotten lost
in the crack at the center
and is hiding down there
in the place where left meets right.

THE WORD-SIFTER
SAILS OFF THE MOUNTAIN

Heading south
over dirt roads and tar,
I make my passes
in all the right zones;
check my speed,
clocked by flying aircraft
at the river, *Pemigewasset.*
Only a slight skid
by the brook—*Skookumchuck?*

More danger
in the lakes region:
mounting steamy hills,
I curve in and out of rain
and the etymological mists
of *Squam,* feeling squeamish;
follow bent arrows and
a new sound —*Winnipesaukee*
(where the Great Spirit smiles);
query squally skypillows
breaking to pieces in the wind—
Nimbus? Fracto-cumulus?

A quick turn
to catch the blur of
black-eyed-Susans at the edge
of a back-hills road (*Thunbergia
alata* in my book of flowers)—
then swivel back to the shock
of an 18-wheeler bearing down on me,
racing to the mill with his load of logs.
A body could lose itself
on a ride like this—
just looking for roots
and taking a turn too wide.

WHAT WILL MY SCRIBBLES SAY?

If I should suddenly die
I guess the kids will clean up;
and I couldn't care less
who gets the Chippendale mirror.
I bet they'll save the sweaters that fit
and sell my old rocking horse
at the flea market!

No doubt my lists will
puzzle them. They puzzle me.
Refrigerator magnets don't hold much
(a missing phrase? a shopping spree?) Coat
pocket holds *a quart of milk, a dozen eggs.*
But daughter, look! There's a poem in my purse;
and the end drawer's secret is my scrawl
from talking to the wolf at 3 AM.

RACCOONS, THE MOST ARTICULATE

Even in dreams these masked hawkers of sound
pad in on slippered feet, gaze at the moon,
sniff their fastidious noses, and tilt their
sensitive silver-tipped ears to catch vibes
too high-pitched or faint for most receivers.

On summer nights, when a bright moonwedge
mirrors itself in their green-gold eyes,
they are trilling and churring songs
that shiver the spine, screeching like owls,
or humming their kits to sleep in tremolos.

In August they watch the corn patch from the woods,
pull down experimental stalks, testing for honey
or gold. Always they know when the ears are ready.
They drink the sweet milk by moonlight—
it dribbles down over their whiskers and tassled chins.

They may be the last voyeurs,
able to see in all directions,
rolling round pebbles between their hands for joy.
Each night they sharpen claws for the prowl,
pausing only to test for scent and sound.

INTO THE RHODODENDRON

Green leaves
only slightly iced,
less tightly clenched

unscrolling,
sufficiently supple
to look like themselves

again? A certain shine
this March morning
could be shimmer

from glass I'm looking through?
or glimmer of greening
leaves in their leaf-shine?

The unscrolling
in me . . . past branches
to earth in its usual brown;

I touch snowless ground,
and flit through this bush
to new bracts: these

incipient, flame-shaped
buds; one per cluster.
Winter has been kind

so far. A branch stirs
and I think it's the wind.
But no...

a small gray bird,
mostly hidden,
with feet like twigs

his grayness
sitting on a branch
in slivers of light

preening his feathers
but mindful
of passing shadows

as I slip away
to gather brushes,
thinking *I'll paint him*

like bamboo,
with simple strokes;
but when I return

he is gone.

DREAMING I AM
JACOB'S LADDER

—*Genesis* 28:12

I dream I am Jacob's ladder,
my feet touching earth,
the top of me reaching to heaven;
and I am glad to be a ladder,
only dazed trying to fathom
my own good fortune
and insignificance. *What am I?*
A bunch of sticks tied together.

Nothing really. Only the means
by which *they* come and go.
I feel their vibrations
and yes! a certain pride as
the slippered feet of the angels of God
ascending and descending
like musical notes in a glissando
touch me there . . . and there.

When the man Jacob appears
and lays his head down
by my bottom-most rung
with a stone for a pillow,
I am speechless . . .
but his words shiver my ribs
and shake my wooden uprights:
Surely the LORD is in this place.

EPILOGUE

CAPTIVA

Some day—when I have forgotten the names
of islands and *Double-Crested Cormorants*
and can only tell you it was a pretty bird
or something that began with C—
when this *Reticulated Cowrie* is just another shell
and the nurse says, "Sorry, lights out!"
before I've finished my memories
or had a chance to read the big-print book
on my lap—if someone would slip me
my old Captiva album, when no one's looking
I'll rock and peel away the plastic wraps,
finger prints and photos; and you can be
sure—even if I can't call it by name—
I'll find this *Hibiscus syriacus*
and kiss its glossy face.

ABOUT THE AUTHOR

JEAN TUPPER has worked as a magazine writer and editor, but her current writing love is poetry. Her work has been published in many fine literary magazines and she is a frequent workshop facilitator and mentor to developing writers. She has been associated with the Fine Line Poets in Massachusetts, and the Wood Thrush Poets, a Connecticut-based group of poets who have been colleagues and friends for 25 years. She has given many readings with these groups, in schools, libraries, and bookstores throughout New England.

A graduate of the Simmons College School of Publication, Jean completed her MA in English at Central Connecticut State University. She has also studied at The Frost Place in Franconia, New Hampshire, the Mt. Holyoke Writers' Conference, and the Fine Arts Work Center in Provincetown, Massachusetts.

While living in Connecticut—until 1990, when she returned to the Boston area—she was a member and secretary of the Connecticut Poetry Society and taught creative writing at New Horizons in Farmington, a unique facility for the physically challenged. She also worked with Services for the Elderly.

Currently, she lives with her husband Russ in Wrentham, Massachusetts, is "Mom" to another poet, Nancy Tupper Ling, and "Nana" to Elizabeth and Sarah.